NATIONAL GEOGRAPHIC

D0503637

Mapping North America

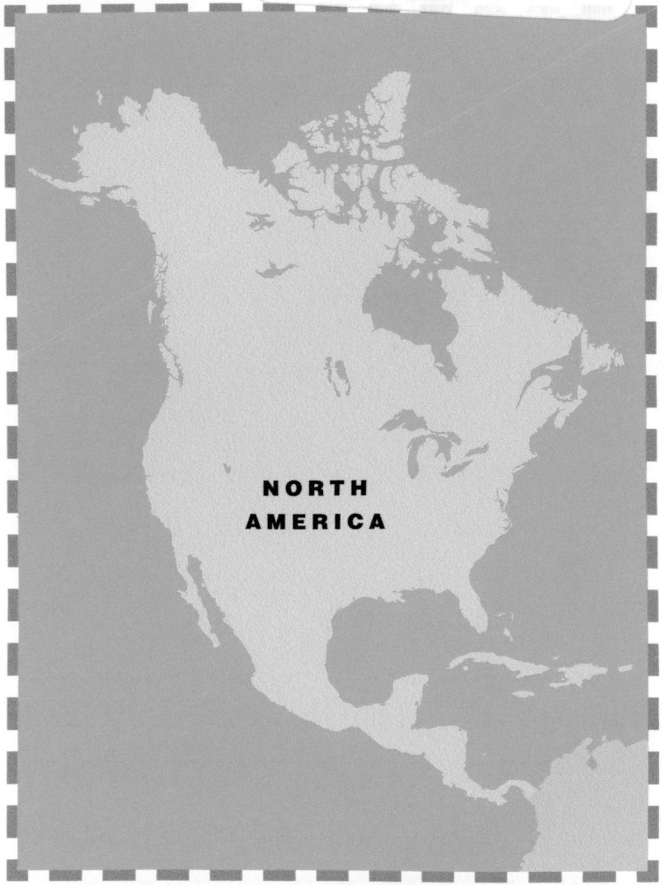

Kate McGough

North America is one of the seven **continents** in the world. This is what a map of North America looks like.

NORTH
AMERICA

There are many lakes in North America.
Lakes look like this on a map.

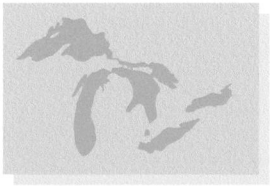

Find the Great Lakes
on the map.

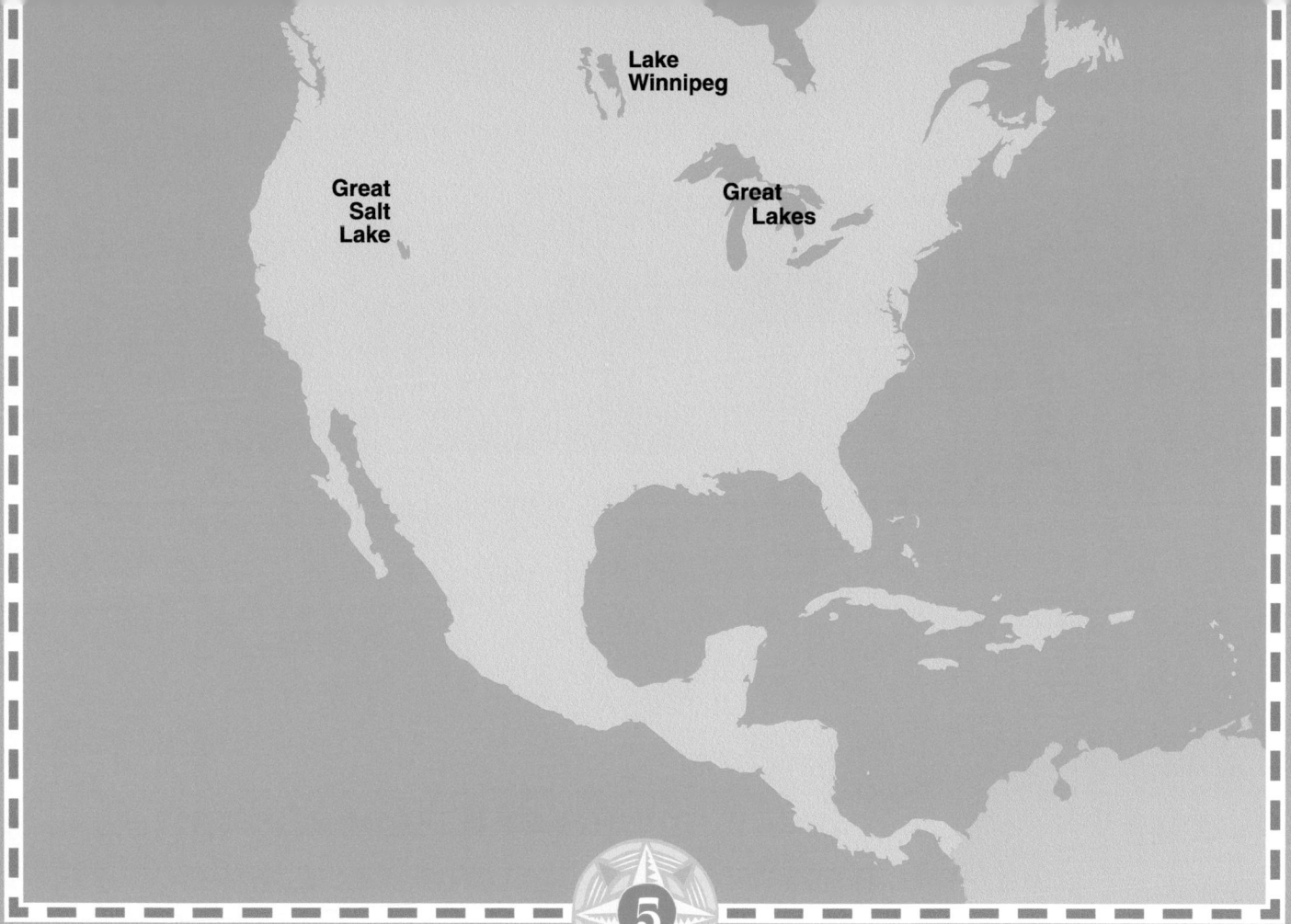
Lake
Winnipeg
Great
Salt
Lake
Great
Lakes

There are many **rivers** in North America.
Rivers look like this on a map.

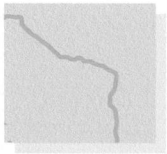

Find the Yukon River
on the map.

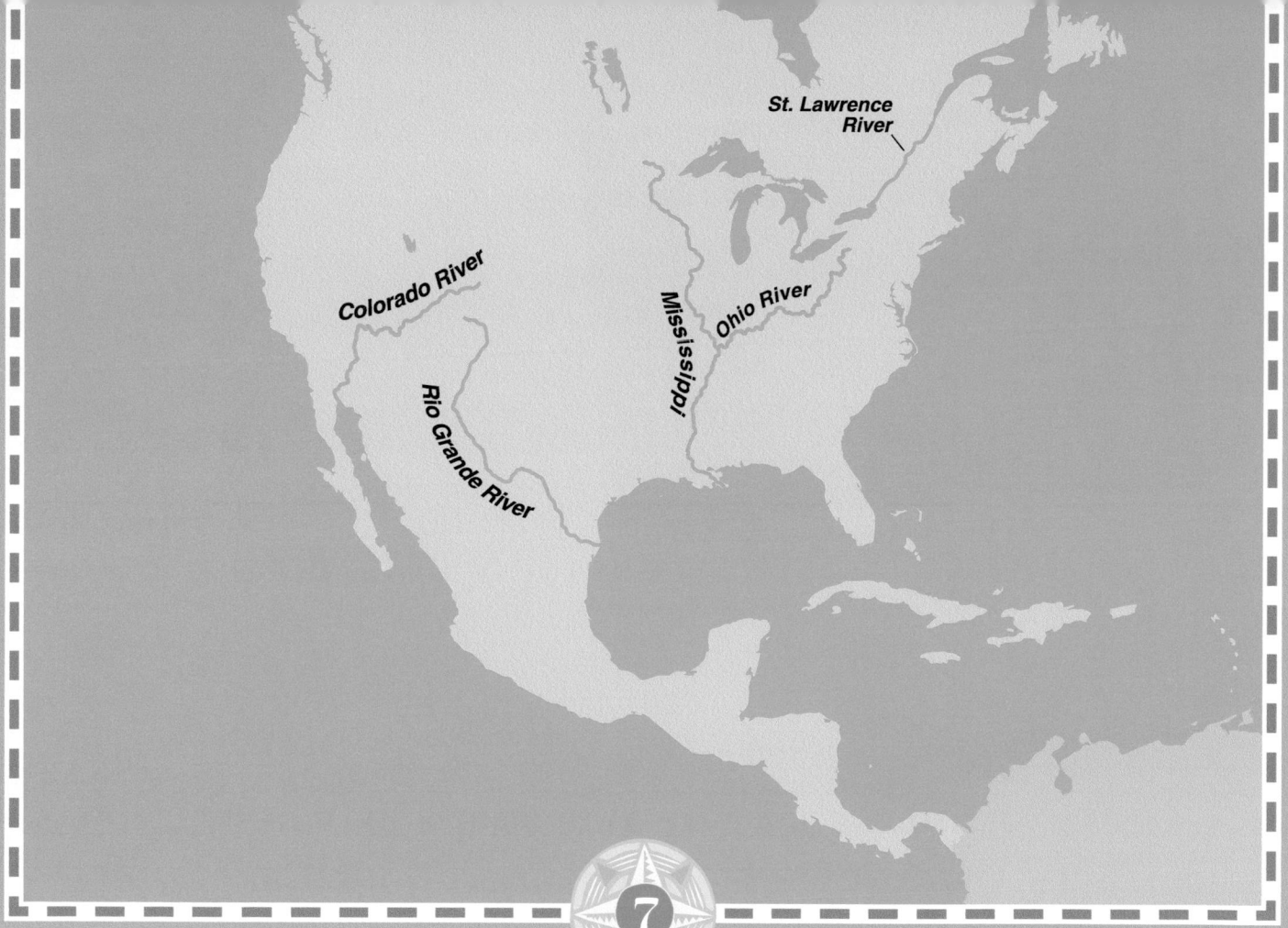
St. Lawrence River
Colorado River
Mississippi
Ohio River
Rio Grande River

There are many **mountain ranges** in North America. Mountain ranges look like this on a map.

Find the Rocky Mountains on the map.

Y MOUNTAINS
SIERRA MADRE
APPALACHIAN MOUNTAINS

There are three **countries** in North America.
Country borders look like this on a map.

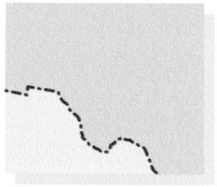

Find Mexico on the map.

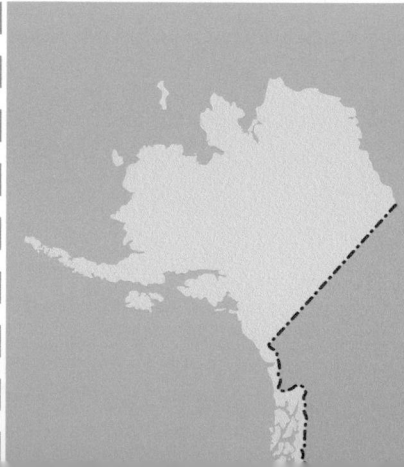

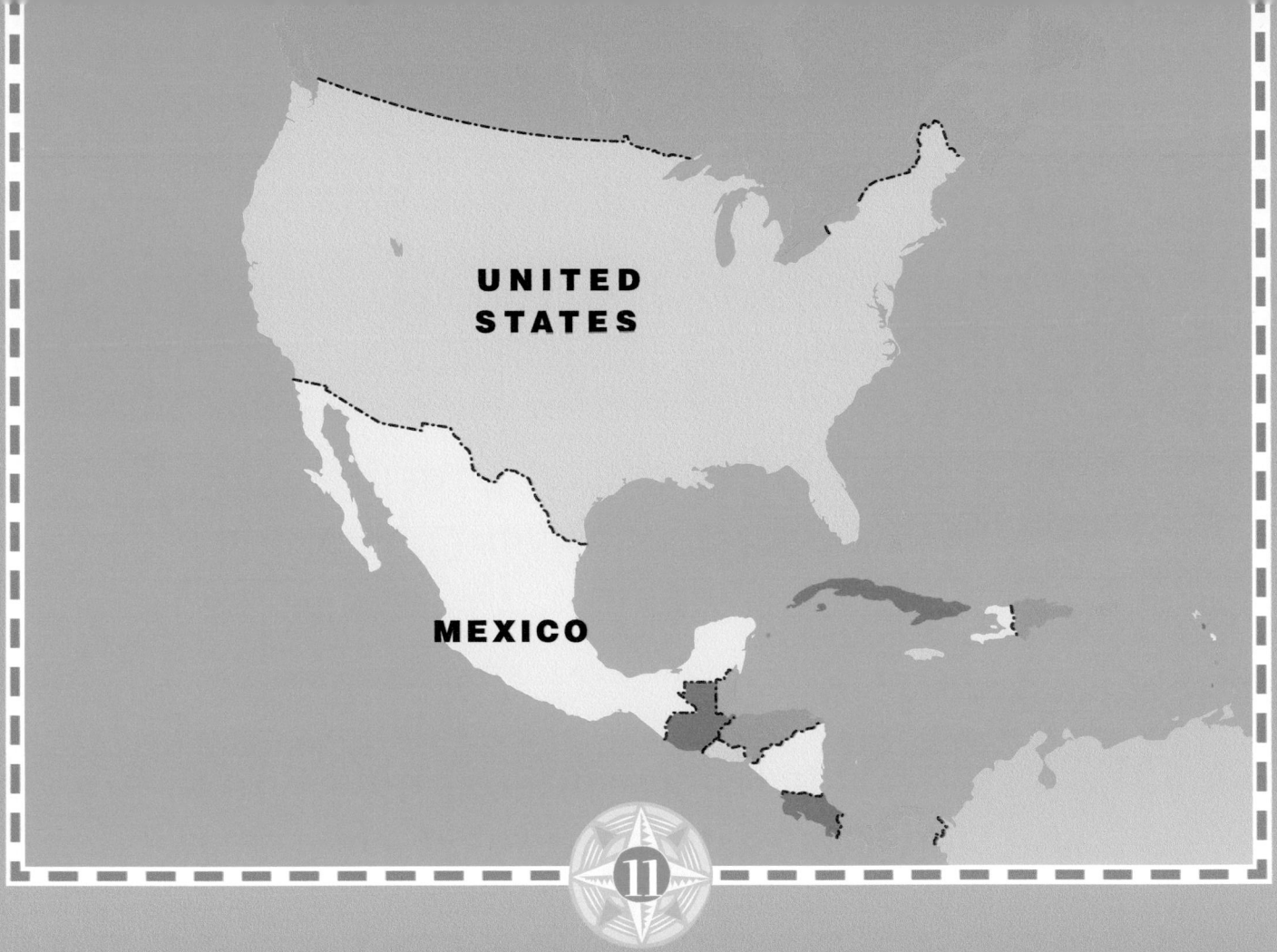
UNITED
STATES
MEXICO

There are many cities in North America.
Cities look like this on a map.

Find New Orleans
on the map.

Vancouver
Ottawa
Chicago
New York
Washington, D.C.
Los Angeles
New Orleans
Miami
Mexico

Look at the map of North America.
Find each of these places:

- Great Salt Lake
- Rio Grande River
- Appalachian Mountains
- Canada
- Vancouver

Vancouver
MOUNTAINS
Lake Winnipeg
St. Lawrence River
Ottawa
Great Lakes
Great Salt Lake
Chicago
New York
UNITED STATES
Mississippi River
Ohio River
APPALACHIAN MOUNTAINS
Washington, D.C.
Colorado River
Los Angeles
Rio Grande River
SIERRA MADRE
New Orleans
Miami
MEXICO
Mexico

Index

cities	13
continents	3
countries	11
lakes	5
mountain ranges	9
rivers	7